American Muscle

Icons of Power and Speed

Etienne Psaila

American Muscle: Icons of Power and Speed

Cover design by Etienne Psaila

Interior layout by Etienne Psaila

Foreword

In the pantheon of automotive culture, few genres capture the imagination and exhilaration like the American muscle car. Born from an era of audacious innovation and fierce competition, these roaring icons of the road have etched an indelible mark on both the asphalt and the heart of car enthusiasts worldwide. This book, a curated journey through the most iconic American muscle cars, is both an ode to their legacy and a visual feast for the aficionado and the newcomer alike.

The muscle car is more than just a vehicle; it's a symbol of a bygone era that celebrated raw power, unbridled performance, and the sheer joy of driving. In these pages, you will find the stories of ingenuity and rivalry that gave birth to these legends on wheels. From the pioneering roar of the 1949 Oldsmobile Rocket 88 to the modern thunder of the Ford Mustang Shelby GT500, each car is a chapter in a saga of technological evolution, cultural impact, and enduring appeal.

As you turn through the pages, you'll encounter a blend of meticulously researched specifications and vibrant photographs that bring these mechanical marvels to life. Every paragraph, every spec table, every image is an invitation to appreciate the nuances that make each model unique - the throaty growl of a V8 engine, the sleek lines of a sculpted body, and the tales of competition and innovation that fueled their creation.

This book is more than just a compilation of cars; it's a journey through time, tracing the evolution of the muscle car from its inception to its modern-day incarnations. It celebrates the spirit of an era where speed and power ruled the streets, and where the car was a canvas for both engineers and dreamers.

So, buckle up and prepare for a ride through history. Whether you're a lifelong enthusiast or new to the world of muscle cars, this book aims to ignite your passion and deepen your appreciation for these incredible machines. Welcome to the thrilling world of American muscle cars - a world where power, performance, and style converge to create something truly spectacular.

1949 Oldsmobile Rocket 88

The 1949 Oldsmobile Rocket 88 is often hailed as the first American muscle car. It marked a significant departure from the conventional cars of its era, thanks to its innovative design and performance. Under the hood, the Rocket 88 featured Oldsmobile's new "Rocket" V8 engine, a high-compression overhead-valve V8 in a relatively lightweight body, an unprecedented combination at the time. This resulted in impressive performance figures, setting a new standard for American cars. Its success in popularizing the muscle car concept was further cemented by its dominance in early NASCAR races, where it quickly became a force to be reckoned with.

Specification	Detail
Engine Type	Rocket V8
Displacement	303 cubic inches (5.0 L)
Horsepower	135 HP at 3600 rpm
Torque	263 lb-ft at 1800 rpm
Transmission	3-speed manual / 4-speed Hydramatic automatic
Body Style	2-door coupe, 2-door sedan, 2-door convertible, 4-door sedan
Top Speed	Approximately 97 mph (156 km/h)
0 to 60 mph	Around 12.2 seconds
Production Years	1949-1957

FUTURAMIC OLDSMOBILE
Station Wagon

1964 Pontiac GTO

The 1964 Pontiac GTO is revered as one of the most iconic muscle cars of all time, marking the beginning of the true muscle car era. Born from the creative work of John DeLorean and his team at Pontiac, the GTO was essentially a performance package for the Pontiac Tempest. The GTO moniker, inspired by the Ferrari 250 GTO, stood for "Gran Turismo Omologato." The car featured a powerful V8 engine, sporty styling, and performance-focused features that appealed to younger buyers. Its introduction sparked a muscle car frenzy in the United States, leading to the development of numerous competitors.

Specification	Detail
Engine Type	389 cubic inches (6.4 L) V8
Horsepower	325 HP (standard); 348 HP (Tri-Power option)
Torque	428 lb-ft
Transmission	3-speed manual (standard); 4-speed manual and 2-speed automatic (optional)
Body Style	2-door coupe, hardtop, and convertible
Top Speed	Approximately 115 mph (185 km/h)
0 to 60 mph	Around 6.6 seconds (with Tri-Power option)
Production Years	1964-1974 (First generation: 1964-1967)

Pontiac Motor Division • General Motors Corporation.

You can get a set of five big, full-color action shots of the GTO, 2+2 and the new OHC Six—suitable for framing. See details below.

To all the other cars from the GTO:

"What's new, pussycats?"

It takes more than a big bore V-8 on a little chassis to make a GTO. The genius of the GTO is that it's the world's greatest compromise. In its proletarian version, it's a very manageable machine. With its 4-barrel carb, standard cam, and firm but civilized suspension, your grandmother can drive it. (Front and rear seat belts are standard. Be sure to tell her to buckle them.) But if you want to start grubbing around in our parts bin and add on our three deuces, one of our close-ratio four speeds and our tach, you can turn your GTO into the famous Gee TO Tiger. Catch one. Wherever real tigers are sold.

Like to have the Wide-Track Tigers prowling your wall? Pontiac will send you five ready-to-frame, 26" x 11½" full-color reproductions of the famous GTO, 2+2 and new OHC Six in action just like you see above—plus a full set of factory specs on all three, plus five GTO emblem decals. Just send 25¢ (35¢ outside USA) to: Wide-Track Tigers, P. O. Box 888A, 196 Wide-Track Blvd., Pontiac, Mich. 48053.

3 Wide-Track Tigers—2+2, GTO and OHC Six

1964 Ford Mustang

The 1964 Ford Mustang, introduced in April of that year, is an iconic vehicle that played a pivotal role in creating the "pony car" class - a term inspired by the Mustang itself. This class of automobile is characterized by affordable, compact, highly styled cars with sporty or performance-oriented features. The Mustang was built on the Ford Falcon's platform, offering both power and style at a price accessible to younger buyers. Its introduction was a phenomenal success, creating a whole new market segment and inspiring a series of competitors.

Specification	Detail
Engine Options	170 cu in (2.8 L) I6, 260 cu in (4.3 L) V8, 289 cu in (4.7 L) V8
Horsepower	101 HP (I6), 164 HP (260 V8), 210 HP (289 V8)
Torque	156 lb-ft (I6), 258 lb-ft (260 V8), 300 lb-ft (289 V8)
Transmission	3-speed manual, 4-speed manual, 3-speed automatic
Body Styles	2-door coupe, 2-door convertible
Top Speed	Approximately 110 mph (177 km/h) for the 289 V8 model
0 to 60 mph	Around 8 seconds (289 V8 model)
Production Years	1964-1973 (First generation)

Presenting
the unexpected...
new Ford Mustang!
$2368* f.o.b. Detroit

1965 Chevrolet Malibu SS

The 1965 Chevrolet Malibu SS represented Chevrolet's entry into the burgeoning muscle car market of the 1960s. Originally a trim level of the Chevrolet Chevelle, the Malibu SS (Super Sport) was distinguished by its added performance features and sporty styling. The '65 model year brought notable changes including a restyled grille and the introduction of the Z16 option, which included a powerful big-block engine. The Malibu SS became popular for its combination of performance, style, and affordability, and it played a significant role in Chevrolet's muscle car lineup.

Specification	Detail
Engine Options	283 cu in (4.6 L) V8, 327 cu in (5.4 L) V8, 396 cu in (6.5 L) Z16 V8 (limited edition)
Horsepower	220 HP (283 V8), up to 350 HP (327 V8), 375 HP (Z16 396 V8)
Torque	Varied by engine option
Transmission	2-speed Powerglide automatic, 3-speed manual, 4-speed manual
Body Styles	2-door coupe, 2-door convertible
Top Speed	Approximately 120 mph (193 km/h) for the Z16 model
0 to 60 mph	Around 6 seconds (Z16 model)
Production Years	1964-1967 (Malibu SS)

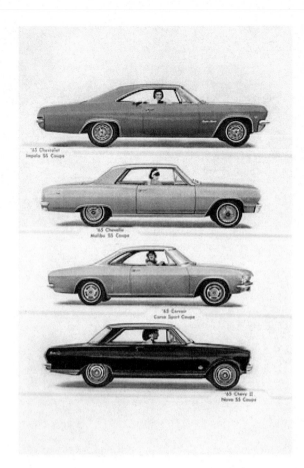

Let Chevrolet put you in beautiful shape for '65

Now, a Chevrolet that makes everything over, under and around you beautifully different. A completely new Corvair with its first big change in five years. A Chevelle that doesn't hold back on anything but cost. And a Chevy II that's turned into the most powerful tightwad in town!

For 1965, the big luxurious Chevrolet could almost get by on looks alone. But that's far from all that's new.

It's longer, lower, roomier, heavier, more luxurious than any Chevrolet before. Completely new from the sleek Impala Super Sport Coupe roof line all the way down to the Jet-smooth suspension.

More expensive looking outside, richer looking inside, more shoulder room, more leg room up front — all in all, we think it's the best Chevrolet we've ever built.

'65 Corvair

Corvair's rear engine has never had so much excitement to look forward to. Inside, there's more shoulder room. More comfort. The effortless handling only a rear engine and new independent suspension can give.

All wrapped up in seven models, including the brand-new top-of-the-line Corsa.

New performance, too—up to 180 hp that you can order in the Corsa Series.

Wait till the ones who always wait till next year see this!

'65 Chevelle

There are enough changes in Chevelle to make it, too, feel like another whole new car from Chevrolet.

New ride, new style, and an engine that will make you feel young again — a 300-hp V8 that you can order in all twelve Chevelles.

And its smoother ride and extra body insulation make things as quiet as the day the kids went back to school.

And if that's too quiet, order an AM-FM Stereo radio.

'65 Chevy II

Our economy is on the upswing!

For '65, Chevy II has a dressed-up front, back, interior and a smart new roof on sedans. Plus two new V8's available: a 250-hp and a 300-hp.

Underlying it, though, are those things that have made Chevy II such a tightwad these past years.

And as your Chevrolet dealer will show you, Chevy II's now the most exciting tightwad in town. . . . Chevrolet Division of General Motors, Detroit, Michigan.

1968 Dodge Charger

The 1968 Dodge Charger stands as a quintessential American muscle car, renowned for its iconic design and powerful performance. This model marked the introduction of the second-generation Charger, featuring a complete design overhaul with a now-famous coke bottle shape, a recessed grille, and hidden headlights that gave it an aggressive, futuristic look. The Charger's popularity was amplified by its appearances in film and television, most notably in the film "Bullitt" and the TV series "The Dukes of Hazzard."

Specification	Detail
Engine Options	318 cu in (5.2 L) V8, 383 cu in (6.3 L) V8, 426 cu in (7.0 L) Hemi V8, 440 cu in (7.2 L) V8
Horsepower	230 HP (318 V8), 335 HP (383 V8), 425 HP (426 Hemi V8), 375 HP (440 V8)
Torque	Varied by engine option
Transmission	3-speed manual (standard), 4-speed manual, 3-speed automatic (optional)
Body Style	2-door coupe
Top Speed	Approximately 130 mph (209 km/h) for the 426 Hemi model
0 to 60 mph	Around 6 seconds (426 Hemi model)
Production Years	1968-1970 (Second generation)

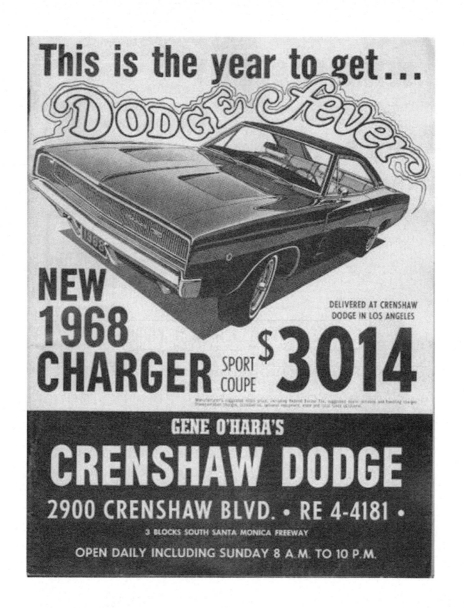

1968 Plymouth Road Runner

The 1968 Plymouth Road Runner was introduced as a unique approach to muscle cars, focusing on performance and affordability. Plymouth designed the Road Runner to be a no-frills, high-performance machine by stripping down the base Belvedere model and equipping it with a powerful engine. The car's name and logo were licensed from Warner Bros., featuring the famous cartoon character, which added a playful and distinctive element to its branding. The Road Runner was an instant hit, offering high performance at a lower cost, and it appealed to a broad audience of driving enthusiasts.

Specification	Detail
Engine Options	383 cu in (6.3 L) V8, 426 cu in (7.0 L) Hemi V8
Horsepower	335 HP (383 V8), 425 HP (426 Hemi V8)
Torque	425 lb-ft (383 V8), 490 lb-ft (426 Hemi V8)
Transmission	3-speed manual (standard), 4-speed manual, 3-speed automatic (optional)
Body Styles	2-door coupe, 2-door hardtop
Top Speed	Approximately 105 mph (169 km/h) for the 383 model
0 to 60 mph	Around 7 seconds (383 V8 model)
Production Years	1968-1980 (First generation: 1968-1970)

1969 Ford Torino Talladega

The 1969 Ford Torino Talladega was a special, high-performance version of the Ford Torino, specifically designed for NASCAR racing. Named after the Talladega Superspeedway, this car was part of Ford's aerodynamics improvement program aimed at dominating high-speed NASCAR tracks. The Torino Talladega featured a sleeker front end with a flush-mounted grille and extended nose, reducing aerodynamic drag. It was built in limited numbers and is now considered a rare collector's item.

Specification	Detail
Engine	428 cu in (7.0 L) Cobra Jet V8
Horsepower	335 HP
Torque	440 lb-ft
Transmission	3-speed automatic, 4-speed manual
Body Style	2-door hardtop
Top Speed	Approximately 140 mph (225 km/h)
0 to 60 mph	Around 6.2 seconds
Production Years	1969 only

1969 Ford Talladega GFT Special

1970 Chevrolet Chevelle SS

The 1970 Chevrolet Chevelle SS (Super Sport) is often celebrated as one of the most iconic and powerful muscle cars ever produced. This model year marked a significant design change for the Chevelle, with a more squared-off, muscular stance, and an aggressive front-end design. The SS package was available with a variety of potent engine options, including the legendary 454 cu in (7.4 L) LS6 V8 engine, which is among the most powerful engines ever put in a production car of that era. The Chevelle SS became a symbol of American muscle car power, known for its brute force and classic styling.

Specification	Detail
Engine Options	396 cu in (6.5 L) V8, 454 cu in (7.4 L) V8 (LS5 and LS6 versions)
Horsepower	350 HP (396 V8), 360 HP (LS5 454 V8), 450 HP (LS6 454 V8)
Torque	415 lb-ft (396 V8), 500 lb-ft (LS5 454 V8), 500 lb-ft (LS6 454 V8)
Transmission	3-speed automatic, 4-speed manual, 2-speed "Powerglide" automatic
Body Styles	2-door coupe, 2-door convertible
Top Speed	Approximately 142 mph (228 km/h) for the LS6 model
0 to 60 mph	Around 6 seconds (LS6 model)
Production Years	1970-1972 (Third generation Chevelle SS)

1970 CHEVROLET

CHEVELLE SS 396 COUPE

Imported direct from USA
and on display at Bill Patterson's showrooms.

Finished in Classic White and Blue with soft vinyl trim. 325 HP
Turbo Jet V8 with Turbo Hydramatic transmission, console shift.
Posi trac rear axle, Power steering, Power windows, tinted glass.
Strato bucket seats, push button radio with rear speaker and many
other features.

BILL PATTERSON HOLDEN 870 4444
Maroondah Highway, Ringwood.
Authorised GM Distributor: Chevrolet - Holden - Torana

After Hours Call Adrian Bowman 723 3894 for full details

1970 Dodge Challenger

The 1970 Dodge Challenger marked Dodge's entry into the pony car market, directly competing with the Chevrolet Camaro and Ford Mustang. Designed to offer a wide range of options, the Challenger was available with an extensive list of trims and engine choices, including the renowned Hemi engines. It stood out with its distinct styling, long hood, and short deck proportions, along with its performance-oriented image. The Challenger quickly became a muscle car icon, celebrated for its power, design, and performance.

Specification	Detail
Engine Options	Wide range including 225 cu in (3.7 L) I6, 318 cu in (5.2 L) V8, 340 cu in (5.6 L) V8, 383 cu in (6.3 L) V8, 426 cu in (7.0 L) Hemi V8, 440 cu in (7.2 L) V8
Horsepower	Ranging from 145 HP (I6) to 425 HP (426 Hemi V8)
Torque	Varied by engine option
Transmission	3-speed automatic, 4-speed manual
Body Styles	2-door coupe, 2-door convertible
Top Speed	Approximately 150 mph (241 km/h) for the 426 Hemi model
0 to 60 mph	Around 6.3 seconds (426 Hemi model)
Production Years	1970-1974 (First generation)

1970 Plymouth Barracuda

The 1970 Plymouth Barracuda represented the dawn of the third generation for this model, showcasing a complete redesign that emphasized a more aggressive and muscular stance. Distancing itself from its previous iterations, the new Barracuda was built on a different platform, leading to a larger and more formidable presence. This model year was particularly notable for offering a wide array of engine choices, including the legendary 426 Hemi V8, making it a favorite among muscle car enthusiasts for its raw power and performance.

Specification	Detail
Engine Options	Ranged from 198 cu in (3.2 L) I6 to 426 cu in (7.0 L) Hemi V8
Horsepower	Up to 425 HP (426 Hemi V8)
Torque	Varied by engine option
Transmission	3-speed automatic, 4-speed manual
Body Styles	2-door coupe, 2-door convertible
Top Speed	Approximately 140 mph (225 km/h) for the Hemi models
0 to 60 mph	Around 5.6 seconds (Hemi models)
Production Years	1970-1974 (Third generation)

1970 Hemi-'Cuda with "Shaker" hood.

Our 1970 Barracudas are totally new. From the plush Barracuda Gran Coupe to the tough little 'Cuda with the Hemi engine.

The Hemi-'Cuda. With a Quivering Cold Air Grabber poking through the hood. So the 426 cubes below can breathe easy.

Very possibly this is the fastest production car in the country.

If you had something gentler, but equally sporty, in mind, we also make Barracuda and the Barracuda Gran Coupe.

So remember the name, new people. Barracuda. It's all yours.

Hello, new people. We have a new car for you.

1970 AMC Rebel "The Machine"

The 1970 AMC Rebel "The Machine" was American Motors Corporation's bold entry into the muscle car arena. It stood out with its patriotic red, white, and blue paint scheme and a powerful 390 cu in (6.4 L) V8 engine. "The Machine" was AMC's performance flagship, featuring a functional "ram-air" hood scoop and heavy-duty suspension. It was designed to be a high-performance vehicle with distinctive styling, capable of competing with the more established muscle cars of its time.

Specification	Detail
Engine	390 cu in (6.4 L) V8
Horsepower	340 HP
Torque	430 lb-ft
Transmission	4-speed manual, 3-speed automatic
Body Style	2-door hardtop
Top Speed	Approximately 125 mph (201 km/h)
0 to 60 mph	Around 6 seconds
Production Years	1970 only

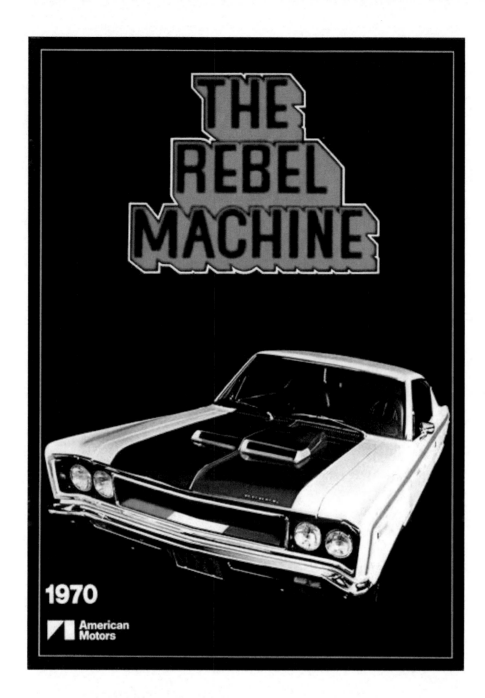

THE REBEL MACHINE

1970

American Motors

1970 Mercury Cougar Eliminator

The 1970 Mercury Cougar Eliminator brought a more performance-focused edge to the Cougar lineup, which was traditionally more luxury-oriented. It featured bold styling, including a blacked-out grille, racing stripes, and a rear spoiler. The Eliminator was available with several potent V8 engine options, including the famed Boss 302 and the 428 Cobra Jet, making it a serious contender in the muscle car segment. It combined Mercury's sophistication with the raw power and agility expected of a muscle car.

Engine Options	302 cu in (4.9 L) V8, 351 cu in (5.8 L) V8, 428 cu in (7.0 L) Cobra Jet V8
Horsepower	290 HP (Boss 302), 300 HP (351 V8), 335 HP (428 Cobra Jet)
Torque	Varied by engine option
Transmission	3-speed automatic, 4-speed manual
Body Style	2-door coupe
Top Speed	Approximately 120 mph (193 km/h) for the Cobra Jet model
0 to 60 mph	Around 7 seconds for the Cobra Jet model
Production Years	1969-1970 (Eliminator model)
Engine Options	302 cu in (4.9 L) V8, 351 cu in (5.8 L) V8, 428 cu in (7.0 L) Cobra Jet V8

MERCURY COUGAR XR7 SUPER PAK.

(Current Series)

428 cubic inch motor with automatic transmission. Radio and stereo tape player. Factory air conditioned. Power sun roof and windows. Dark ivory green. Negligible mileage. Leasing available if desired.

This is the managing director's personal car.

All enquiries to: Paul Jackson,

RON HODGSON MOTORS

Corner Church and Boundary Streets, Parramatta.
Phone 637 7000.

Mercury—Password for Action
1970 Cougar Eliminator / Cyclone Spoiler
Cyclone

1970 Buick GSX

The 1970 Buick GSX was Buick's answer to the muscle car craze, a high-performance version of the already potent Gran Sport (GS) model. The GSX package included a more powerful engine, a heavy-duty suspension, and distinctive, sporty styling with a full-body stripe and rear spoiler. It was most famously available in two eye-catching colors: Saturn Yellow and Apollo White. The GSX, particularly with the Stage 1 engine option, was one of the most powerful muscle cars of its era.

Specification	Detail
Engine Options	455 cu in (7.5 L) V8, including a high-performance Stage 1 option
Horsepower	350 HP (standard 455), 360 HP (Stage 1)
Torque	510 lb-ft (standard 455), 510 lb-ft (Stage 1)
Transmission	3-speed automatic, 4-speed manual
Body Style	2-door coupe
Top Speed	Approximately 115 mph (185 km/h)
0 to 60 mph	Around 6.5 seconds (Stage 1 model)
Production Years	1970 only (GSX package)

MEET A BRAND-NEW BRAND OF BUICK... GSX

HOOD TACH!

BILLBOARDS!

SPOILERS!

SPORTS MIRRORS!

4-SPEED BOX!

BUCKETS!

455-4!

MORE! MORE! MORE!

1971 Dodge Super Bee

The 1971 Dodge Super Bee was a more affordable but no less potent version of Dodge's muscle car lineup. Based on the Dodge Coronet, the Super Bee was designed as a high-performance machine with a lower price tag. The 1971 model year brought in a new, more aerodynamic design with a split grille and a slightly revised rear. The Super Bee was known for its powerful engine options and its distinctive bumblebee stripe around the tail.

Specification	Detail
Engine Options	383 cu in (6.3 L) V8, 440 cu in (7.2 L) V8, 426 cu in (7.0 L) Hemi V8
Horsepower	300 HP (383 V8), 370 HP (440 V8), 425 HP (426 Hemi V8)
Torque	Varied by engine option
Transmission	3-speed automatic, 4-speed manual
Body Style	2-door coupe
Top Speed	Varied by engine option
0 to 60 mph	Around 6.5 seconds (426 Hemi V8 model)
Production Years	1968-1971

CHARGER Super Bee
Even with a 383 Magnum...it's a regular gas.

Hey, man. It's easy to own a super set of wheels if you have a super budget to feed it with, Check?

On the other hand, if you think about it for a while, maybe you could find another place to use the green. If you had some left over. And here's how you get it.

Super Bee, the great-looking piece of man's iron that knows how to live on a budget. Start with a 383 Magnum that's learned to like regular. Plus a power-to-weight ratio that combines handling, stopping, and the ability to leave quickly. Add heavy-duty suspension, super brakes, F70 x 14 bias-belted skins, and the floor-mounted full-synchro three-speed. That's some motor.

And boy, is it great when you have enough left over to take it out Saturday nights. There are a lot of nice, good-thinking reasons to buy a Super Bee. So ignore the fact that it looks like tomorrow and runs like it's all down hill.

Sure you will.

STANDARD EQUIPMENT

383 Magnum V8 (uses regular fuel) □ Performance hood with blackout treatment □ Ventless door glass (43" radius) □ Simulated wood-grained door trim panel inserts, instrument panel applique and Rallye Instrument Cluster with 150-mph speedometer and oil pressure gauge □ Heater/windshield defroster with 3-speed fan □ Carpeting □ Rallye Suspension Package (includes heavy-duty torsion bars, heavy-duty rear springs, sway bar, and heavy-duty shock absorbers) □ 3-speed fully synchronized transmission with floor shift □ Heavy-duty brakes: 11" x 3", front; 11" x 2½", rear □ F70x14 wide-tread, white sidewall, bias-belted tires □ Dual exhausts.

Racing mirror

Bright exhaust tips

Rallye wheel and E60 tire

Pistol grip

1982 Chevrolet Camaro Z28

The 1982 Chevrolet Camaro Z28 represented a significant overhaul for the Camaro line, ushering in the third generation of this iconic pony car. The Z28 model was the high-performance variant, showcasing a modern, sleeker body design, improved handling, and aerodynamics. It was lighter than its predecessors and was equipped with a range of V8 engines, catering to a growing demand for performance along with fuel efficiency. The 1982 Z28 earned the title of Motor Trend's Car of the Year for its advancements and overall performance.

Specification	Detail
Engine Options	305 cu in (5.0 L) V8 (standard), Cross-Fire Injection V8 (optional)
Horsepower	145 HP (standard V8), 165 HP (Cross-Fire Injection V8)
Torque	Varied by engine option
Transmission	4-speed manual, 3-speed automatic
Body Style	2-door coupe
Top Speed	Approximately 110 mph (177 km/h)
0 to 60 mph	Around 9 seconds
Production Years	1982-1992 (Third generation Camaro)

1982 Chevy Camaro Z/28
Indy Pace Car
On loan from Scott Cournoyer of Elk Grove, California

Camaro Is The Best Because...
Camaro was chosen to be the 1982 Indy 500 Pace Car, the third time Camaro was so honored. Two actual pace cars were built for the race and 6,360 replicas were built for sale to the public. All pace cars wore special silver/blue paint and interiors. A special graphics package and Z/28 drivetrain were included.

About This Camaro...
The 1982 Camaro was the third generation of the popular pony car, and the first to feature a hatch back body design. The '82 model was also the first to offer the option of fuel injection and, a sign of the times, a four-cylinder engine. The Z/28 came standard with a 5 liter (305 cu. in.) V-8 with carburetion but offered an optional LU5 5 liter engine with "Cross Fire Injection", an option featured on this car. The Z/28 carried special bodywork and trim, which included a lightweight fiberglass (SMC) hood with a functional cold air intake on LU5-equipped cars. This particular car also features the J65 four-wheel disk brake option. Modifications to the suspension and a reduction of some 470 pounds from the previous generation made the Camaro one of the best handling cars of its time.

Technical... Engine: V-8, OHV, 305 cu. in., 165 hp. Transmission: Three-speed automatic. Brakes: Front/rear disks. Weight: 3,362 lbs. Original price: $9,700 (Z/28 package)

1982 Pontiac Firebird Trans Am

The 1982 Pontiac Firebird Trans Am kicked off the third generation of the Firebird lineup, showcasing a complete redesign that embraced a more aerodynamic and futuristic look. This model was significantly lighter and more streamlined compared to its predecessor, contributing to better fuel efficiency and handling. The Trans Am variant was the performance-oriented model of the lineup, known for its distinctive styling and the iconic 'bird' decal on the hood in some versions. It gained fame as KITT in the TV show "Knight Rider," further cementing its place in pop culture.

Horsepower	Ranged from 145 HP to 200 HP depending on engine and configuration
Torque	Varied by engine option
Transmission	4-speed manual, 3-speed automatic, 5-speed manual
Body Style	2-door coupe
Top Speed	Approximately 115 mph (185 km/h)
0 to 60 mph	Around 9 seconds
Production Years	1982-1992 (Third generation Firebird)
Horsepower	Ranged from 145 HP to 200 HP depending on engine and configuration
Torque	Varied by engine option

YOUR TIME HAS COME

1982 TRANS AM

The excitement began 15 years ago when those electrifying "Birds" came down like rolling thunder to capture the hearts of enthusiasts everywhere. And a legend was born.

Now comes the road machine that will fire-up a new generation!

From saber-like nose to rakish tail, Trans Am is a brilliant orchestration of aerodynamic function. Its .31 drag coefficient is the best of any production car GM has ever tested.

But the new Trans Am is much more than a beautiful piece of automotive sculpture. It's a

THE DRIVER'S CAR

The makings of a legend:
- 5.0 liter 4-bbl. V-8 with dual free-flow resonator exhausts
- 4-speed manual transmission
- Quick-ratio power steering
- MacPherson front struts
- Front and rear stabilizer bars
- Torque arm rear suspension
- Turbo cast aluminum wheels
- P205/70R14 steel radials
- 14½" Formula steering wheel
- Reclining front bucket seats

driver's car that's totally engineered for serious roadwork.

Trans Am with options shown, $10,076. Trans Am's base price? Only $9,659! This is a manufacturer's suggested retail price including dealer prep. Taxes, license, destination charges and optional equipment additional.

One "hands-on" impression will convince you that Trans Am is a driving sensation!

The legend makers at Pontiac have done it again!

Some Pontiacs are equipped with engines produced by other GM divisions, subsidiaries, or affiliated companies worldwide. See your Pontiac dealer for details.

PONTIAC ▼ NOW THE EXCITEMENT REALLY BEGINS

1987 Buick GNX

The 1987 Buick GNX was a high-performance version of the Buick Grand National, developed in partnership with McLaren Performance Technologies/ASC. It was created as a limited production run to mark the end of the rear-wheel-drive Regal line. The GNX (Grand National Experimental) was known for its understated, menacing appearance and a turbocharged V6 engine that offered exceptional performance, rivaling that of many V8-powered cars of its time. Its impressive acceleration and unique status have made the GNX a highly sought-after collector's item.

Specification	Detail
Engine	3.8 L Turbocharged V6
Horsepower	276 HP (officially, though often thought to be underestimated)
Torque	360 lb-ft
Transmission	4-speed automatic
Body Style	2-door coupe
Top Speed	Approximately 124 mph (200 km/h)
0 to 60 mph	Around 5.5 seconds
Production Quantity	547 units

A HIGH-PERFORMANCE INVESTMENT FOR THE FORTUNATE 500.

BUICK GNX.

2004 Pontiac GTO

The 2004 Pontiac GTO marked the revival of the GTO nameplate after several decades. This modern iteration of the GTO was a departure from its classic predecessors, based on the Australian Holden Monaro platform. It was designed to blend modern performance with a nod to its muscle car heritage. The car came equipped with a powerful LS1 V8 engine and offered a balanced mix of performance, comfort, and styling, though it featured a more subdued design compared to the aggressive muscle cars of the past.

Specification	Detail
Engine	5.7 L LS1 V8
Horsepower	350 HP
Torque	365 lb-ft
Transmission	4-speed automatic, 6-speed manual
Body Style	2-door coupe
Top Speed	Approximately 155 mph (250 km/h)
0 to 60 mph	Around 5.3 seconds
Production Years	2004-2006

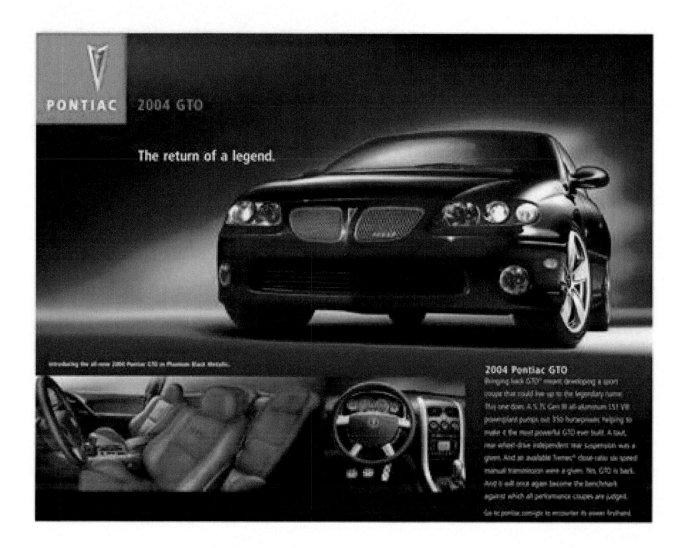

PONTIAC 2004 GTO

The return of a legend.

Introducing the all-new 2004 Pontiac GTO in Phantom Black Metallic.

2004 Pontiac GTO

Bringing back GTO meant developing a sport coupe that could live up to the legendary name. But one does. A 5.7L Gen III all-aluminum LS1 V8 powerplant pumps out 350 horsepower, helping to make it the most powerful GTO ever built. A taut, rear-wheel-drive independent rear suspension was a given. And an available Tremec close-ratio six-speed manual transmission were a given. Yes, GTO is back. And it will once again become the benchmark against which all performance coupes are judged.

Go to pontiac.com/gto to encounter its power firsthand.

2005 Ford Mustang GT

The 2005 Ford Mustang GT heralded the debut of the fifth generation of the Mustang. This model marked a return to the classic Mustang styling cues with a modern twist, often referred to as "retro-futurism." The GT version was equipped with a powerful V8 engine and was praised for its improved performance, handling, and build quality over previous models. It successfully blended nostalgia with contemporary technology, reigniting interest in the Mustang among both new and longtime enthusiasts.

Specification	Detail
Engine	4.6 L Modular V8
Horsepower	300 HP
Torque	320 lb-ft
Transmission	5-speed manual, 5-speed automatic
Body Style	2-door coupe, 2-door convertible
Top Speed	Approximately 149 mph (240 km/h)
0 to 60 mph	Around 5.1 seconds
Production Years	2005-2010 (Fifth generation Mustang)

GIVE US YOUR UNTAMED, YOUR ASSERTIVE,
YOUR LEADFOOTS YEARNING TO BE FREE.

MUSTANG
Built for the road ahead.

2008 Dodge Challenger SRT8

The 2008 Dodge Challenger SRT8 marked the return of the Challenger nameplate after a long hiatus, initiating the third generation of the model. This modern version paid homage to the classic 1970 Challenger with its retro-inspired design. The SRT8 variant was the high-performance model, equipped with a powerful Hemi V8 engine. It combined modern muscle car performance with nostalgic design elements, appealing to both new buyers and muscle car enthusiasts from the original Challenger era.

Specification	Detail
Engine	6.1 L Hemi V8
Horsepower	425 HP
Torque	420 lb-ft
Transmission	5-speed automatic
Body Style	2-door coupe
Top Speed	Approximately 170 mph (274 km/h)
0 to 60 mph	Around 4.9 seconds
Production Years	2008-present (Third generation Challenger)

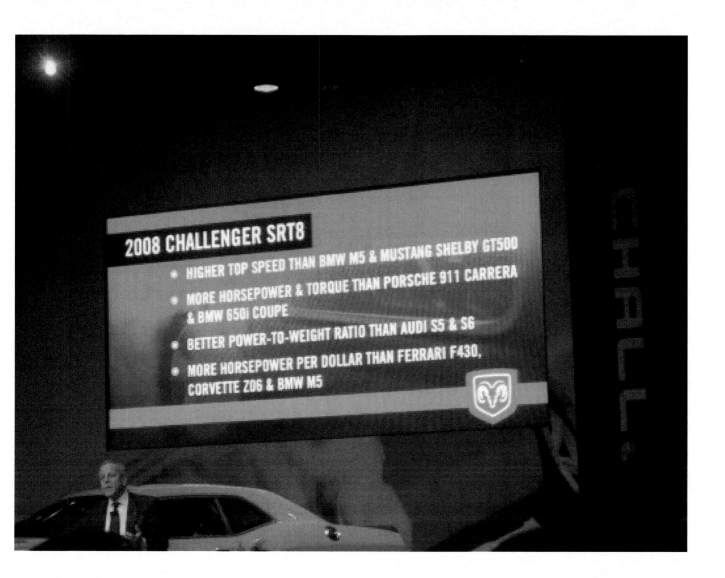

2009 Chevrolet Camaro SS

The 2009 Chevrolet Camaro SS was a part of the much-anticipated reintroduction of the Camaro, beginning the fifth generation. The SS model was the performance-oriented version, combining a muscular and aggressive design with a potent V8 engine. This new Camaro was a modern interpretation of the classic Camaro styling, featuring advanced technology and improved performance dynamics, successfully reviving the Camaro's legacy in the modern muscle car market.

Engine	6.2 L LS3 V8 (manual), 6.2 L L99 V8 (automatic)
Horsepower	426 HP (LS3), 400 HP (L99)
Torque	420 lb-ft (LS3), 410 lb-ft (L99)
Transmission	6-speed manual, 6-speed automatic
Body Style	2-door coupe, 2-door convertible
Top Speed	Approximately 155 mph (250 km/h)
0 to 60 mph	Around 4.6 seconds (LS3)
Production Years	2010-present (Fifth generation Camaro)
Engine	6.2 L LS3 V8 (manual), 6.2 L L99 V8 (automatic)

It wins the beauty contest...
And the strongman competition.

Introducing the *2010 Chevrolet Camaro*. To compliment it's stunning exterior design, this new generation muscle car has the best in class horsepower, torque and Mile Per Gallon (MPG) numbers when compared to Mustang and Challenger. Looking back at the original 1967 pony car...Some things never change.

www.gm.ca

2012 Chevrolet Camaro ZL1

The 2012 Chevrolet Camaro ZL1 raised the bar for the Camaro lineup, introducing a supercharged V8 engine that made it one of the most powerful production cars of its time. The ZL1 was designed not just for straight-line speed but also for impressive handling and braking performance, making it a well-rounded performance car. It featured advanced technologies like magnetic ride suspension and was a significant step up from the already potent SS model, offering track-ready capabilities in a street-legal package.

Specification	Detail
Engine	6.2 L Supercharged LSA V8
Horsepower	580 HP
Torque	556 lb-ft
Transmission	6-speed manual, 6-speed automatic
Body Style	2-door coupe, 2-door convertible
Top Speed	Approximately 184 mph (296 km/h)
0 to 60 mph	Around 3.9 seconds
Production Years	2012-present (Fifth generation Camaro)

2015 Dodge Charger Hellcat

The 2015 Dodge Charger Hellcat was introduced as one of the most powerful sedans in the world, thanks to its supercharged 6.2-liter Hemi V8 engine. This version of the Charger was part of the seventh generation and stood out for its extraordinary power combined with four-door practicality. The Charger Hellcat offered exceptional straight-line speed, aggressive styling, and modern technology, making it a unique blend of family sedan functionality and supercar-like performance.

Specification	Detail
Engine	6.2 L Supercharged Hemi V8
Horsepower	707 HP
Torque	650 lb-ft
Transmission	8-speed automatic
Body Style	4-door sedan
Top Speed	Approximately 204 mph (328 km/h)
0 to 60 mph	Around 3.6 seconds
Production Years	2015-present (Seventh generation Charger)

2020 Ford Mustang Shelby GT500

The 2020 Ford Mustang Shelby GT500 is the most powerful production Mustang ever created. It represents the pinnacle of Mustang performance, combining a supercharged V8 engine with advanced aerodynamics and track-focused technology. The GT500 carries on the legacy of Carroll Shelby's original high-performance Mustangs, offering an exhilarating driving experience with modern technology and design. It's a car designed for both the track and the road, showcasing the evolution of the Mustang into a world-class sports car.

Specification	Detail
Engine	5.2 L Supercharged V8
Horsepower	760 HP
Torque	625 lb-ft
Transmission	7-speed dual-clutch automatic
Body Style	2-door coupe
Top Speed	Approximately 180 mph (290 km/h)
0 to 60 mph	Around 3.3 seconds
Production Years	2020-present (Sixth generation Mustang)

Ford Mustang RTR Spec 3

The Ford Mustang RTR Spec 3 is a specialty version of the Ford Mustang, created by RTR Vehicles. RTR, which stands for "Ready to Rock," is a venture by professional drifter Vaughn Gittin Jr. The Spec 3 package is a comprehensive upgrade over the base Mustang, including enhancements to both performance and aesthetics. It features a supercharged version of the Mustang's V8 engine, along with suspension upgrades, custom wheels, and distinctive RTR styling elements, making it a standout choice for enthusiasts looking for something beyond the standard Mustang offerings.

Specification	Detail
Engine	Supercharged 5.0 L V8
Horsepower	Over 700 HP
Torque	Not specified
Transmission	6-speed manual or 10-speed automatic
Body Style	2-door coupe
Top Speed	Not officially specified
0 to 60 mph	Estimated under 4 seconds
Special Features	RTR body kit, suspension upgrades, custom wheels

Hennessey Exorcist

The Hennessey Exorcist is a highly modified version of the Chevrolet Camaro ZL1, created by Hennessey Performance Engineering. It was developed as a direct response to the Dodge Challenger SRT Demon. The Exorcist package significantly boosts the power of the ZL1's supercharged V8 engine and includes numerous performance enhancements designed to improve the car's speed and handling. The Exorcist is a limited-production vehicle, with Hennessey aiming to create a muscle car capable of exceptional straight-line performance, capable of competing with the world's fastest supercars.

Specification	Detail
Engine	Upgraded Supercharged 6.2 L V8
Horsepower	1,000 HP
Torque	883 lb-ft
Transmission	6-speed manual or 10-speed automatic
Body Style	2-door coupe
Top Speed	Approximately 217 mph (349 km/h)
0 to 60 mph	Estimated under 3 seconds
Production	Limited production

Dodge Challenger SRT Demon

The Dodge Challenger SRT Demon is a highly specialized, limited-production version of the Challenger, created for unmatched straight-line acceleration. Launched in 2018, it's one of the fastest production cars in the world in terms of 0 to 60 mph and quarter-mile times. The Demon includes numerous drag racing-specific features and holds the distinction of being the first production car to lift the front wheels during acceleration. It's powered by a supercharged 6.2-liter Hemi V8, heavily modified from the Hellcat version, and it was marketed as the ultimate drag racing muscle car.

Specification	Detail
Engine	Supercharged 6.2 L Hemi V8
Horsepower	808 HP (840 HP with 100 octane fuel)
Torque	717 lb-ft (770 lb-ft with 100 octane fuel)
Transmission	8-speed automatic
Body Style	2-door coupe
Top Speed	Limited to 168 mph (270 km/h) due to tires
0 to 60 mph	2.3 seconds
Quarter Mile	9.65 seconds at 140 mph (225 km/h)

Conclusion

As we close the pages on this exploration of American muscle cars, from their roaring beginnings in the 1960s to the astonishingly powerful machines of the 21st century, we are left to ponder the future of this iconic segment of the automotive world. The question that looms large is: Will the American muscle car embrace the inevitable shift towards hybrid and electric powertrains?

Muscle car culture, with its deep roots in raw horsepower, throaty V8 engines, and the rumble of exhaust, might seem at odds with the quiet, eco-friendly nature of electric vehicles (EVs). However, the automotive industry's landscape is rapidly changing, driven by advancements in technology and increasing environmental concerns. Electrification is not just a trend; it's becoming a necessity, and even the bastions of traditional muscle are not immune to this shift.

The potential for hybrid and electric muscle cars is immense. Electric motors can deliver instant torque, a key component of the muscle car's appeal, potentially offering acceleration that surpasses even the most potent internal combustion engines. Moreover, the integration of electric powertrains doesn't mean the abandonment of what makes a muscle car a muscle car. Instead, it's an evolution, a way to adapt and embrace new technologies while retaining the essence of what these cars represent: power, performance, and a rebellious spirit.

Manufacturers like Ford, Chevrolet, and Dodge have already begun to integrate electric technology into their lineups. Ford's Mustang Mach-E, an all-electric SUV, hints at the possibilities, blending the Mustang's heritage with an entirely electric future. The key will be in how well these new-age muscle cars balance tradition with innovation, maintaining the visceral appeal that has defined them for decades.

In conclusion, the future of the American muscle car may very well be electric, but it's unlikely to lose its soul in the process. Instead, it will evolve, embracing new technologies to create a new era of high-performance vehicles. These future muscle cars will likely pay homage to their storied past while blazing a trail into a high-octane, electrified future. The rumble of a V8 may give way to the whirr of electric motors, but the spirit of the American muscle car will continue to thrive, embodying the relentless pursuit of power and freedom on the open road.

About the Author

Etienne Psaila: An Accomplished Author and Educator

With a writing journey spanning two decades, Etienne Psaila has long been passionate about crafting stories. For many years, he wrote purely for the pleasure it brought, sharing his works exclusively with a close circle of friends and family. It was only recently, spurred by the enthusiastic feedback from his readers, that he ventured into the realm of publishing. Today, his works are available in various formats, from eBooks to paperbacks.

Etienne holds a Bachelor of Education degree from the prestigious University of Malta. For the past 20 years, he has devoted himself to the noble profession of teaching. His commitment to education is evident not only in the classroom but also in the written word, as he occasionally authors short stories tailored for his students. He firmly believes that his teaching experiences enrich his storytelling, offering a unique perspective that sets his work apart.

Diverse in his literary pursuits, Etienne delves into various genres, ranging from historical and romantic fiction to thrillers and science fiction. Recognizing the ever-evolving reading habits in our fast-paced world, he also pens concise narratives, perfect for a two or three-sitting read. These shorter tales serve as an ideal alternative for those who might not have the time to immerse themselves in lengthier novels and for those seeking a break from the constant influx of social media. Whether long or short, fiction or non-fiction, Etienne's books cater to a wide audience.

Currently, Etienne calls the beautiful island nation of Malta home.

Printed in Great Britain
by Amazon

34657151R10064